Arnold Saves the Day

Written by Jenny Feely

Illustrated by Steve Axelsen

Flying Start
to Literacy®

T0363482

CONTENTS

Chapter 1
A hard time for Arnold

Every day all the animals were
nasty to Arnold.

Arnold was an anteater. He had
a long, sticky tongue. Every day he
dug into ant nests with his sharp
claws. He licked up the ants with
his tongue and ate them.

"How can you eat all those poor little ants?" said the other animals.

"It's my job," said Arnold. "And it's very important."

"It's disgusting!" the giraffe said,
as she wrapped her long, long
tongue around some thorny branches
to get the soft green leaves she ate.

"We agree," said the beavers,
as they chewed their way through
some woody logs.

And the hummingbird ignored
Arnold as she fed in the nearby
trees.

"You are revolting!" they all
said together.

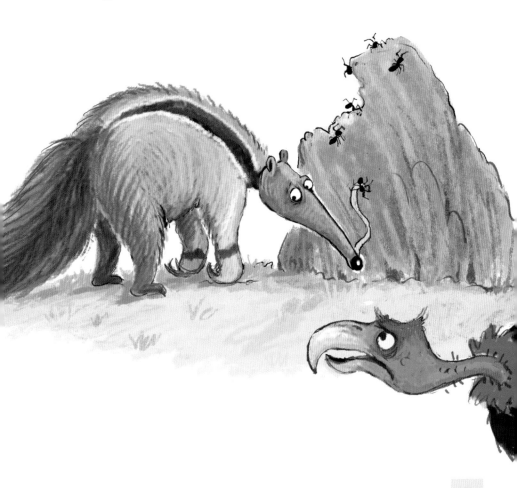

Arnold looked at the spider, the
vulture and the vampire bat.

The spider was sucking up the
juices of a grasshopper.
The vulture was eating
a dead animal.

And when the giraffe wasn't
looking, the bat was sucking some
blood from her neck.

"Eating ants is disgusting!" said all
the animals as they looked down
at Arnold. "How can you do it?"

Chapter 2
Not a friend in sight

This was all too much for Arnold.
He stopped scratching at the ant
nest and sat down. A big tear
rolled down his face.

"No one likes me," said Arnold.
"I have no friends. And it is all
because I eat ants. What will
I do?"

Arnold sobbed and sobbed. None
of the animals took any notice.

Then Arnold had an idea.

Arnold turned and looked
at the other animals.

"You don't like me eating ants?"
he asked.

"We don't,"
they all said.

"Well," said Arnold. "I will stop
eating ants. I will find something
else to eat. I will be more like you."

"That is an excellent idea,"
said the other animals.

Chapter 3
Trouble at dinner time

The next day Arnold didn't try to scratch his way into ant nests and he didn't eat any ants.

Arnold decided to eat some leaves like the giraffe did. Arnold climbed up a thorny tree.

But Arnold's claws got in the way. He lost his grip and came tumbling down.

"This is no good," said Arnold. "I must try something else."

Arnold tried collecting nectar from
flowers like the hummingbird did.

Arnold's tongue could reach inside
the flowers to collect the nectar,
but the pollen in the flowers made
him sneeze.

"Ahh–choo! Ahh–choo!"
Arnold couldn't stop sneezing.

"This isn't working," he said.

Arnold tried eating a woody log
like the beavers did, but splinters
of wood stuck to his tongue.

Arnold was getting hungrier and
hungrier.

Chapter 4
The trouble with ants

The other animals didn't notice that Arnold was having a hard time. They were happy that they didn't have to watch Arnold flicking out his tongue to eat all those poor ants.

But soon they noticed something else. There were ants everywhere!

The ants took all the nectar from the flowers. There was no nectar left for the hummingbird.

The leaves on the thorny tree were covered in ants. When the giraffe tried to eat the leaves, she got a mouthful of ants.

"How disgusting," she said.

When the beavers tried to cut
down a tree, the ants swarmed all
over them.   And the ants crawled
all over the bat and the spider.

"Get off!   Get off!" they all yelled.
"Someone must get rid of these ants."

Chapter 5
Arnold saves the day

All the animals looked at Arnold,
and Arnold looked at all the animals.

"Quick! Start eating all the ants
again," said the hummingbird.

"But you don't like me when
I eat ants," said Arnold.
"You complain about it."

"We're sorry," said all the animals.

"You are the only one who is any good at eating ants," said the giraffe.

"It is very important that there are not too many ants," said the beavers. "Please stop trying to be like us and be yourself."

So Arnold happily went back to doing what all anteaters do best – he ate ants.

And from that day on, all the other animals smiled when they saw Arnold flicking out his tongue and eating ants.